I0440289

> **DEDICATION:**
> This book is dedicated to my
> parents, **Otis and Jewel Daves;**
> my charming older brother;
> **Dr. Maxion Daves;**
> my two lovable children,
> **Albert Cousins & Lucy Simpson,**
> and to my handsome, supportive,
> and funny husband,
> **Dr. David J. Goodwill,**
> without whom this book would not
> have been possible.

Copyright 2011, Dr. Sharon D. Goodwill

Published By Magna Carta
– Sharon & David Goodwill

Photographs by Dr. Sharon D. Goodwill

Printed in the United States of America

First Edition, 2011

Title ID: **3580609**
ISBN-13: **978-1461005339**

My mother was the most beautiful woman I ever saw. All I am I owe to my mother. I attribute all my success in life to the moral, intellectual and physical education I received from her.

-- *George Washington and Sharon Daves Goodwill*

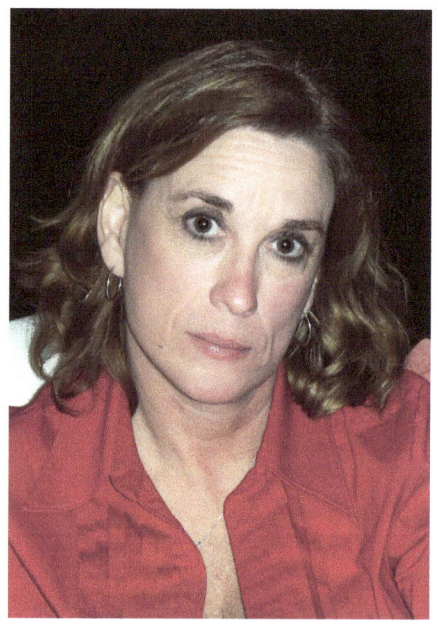

Dr. Sharon Daves Goodwill,
Left-handed Author, Photographer, RN, Teacher, Principal, Director, Scientist, Friend, Aunt, Sister, Daughter, Wife, and Mother.

January 1st
You don't have to be perfect, but you have to be the best that you can be.....

January 2nd
You can never love someone too much...only too little.

January 3rd
Tomorrow is another day.... but today is a day, too... don't waste it.

January 4th
Never settle for less.... strive for more.

January 5th
If you do not like his mother.... in five years, you will not like him either.

January 6th
Never wear clothing that requires explanations to those who see you wear it.

January 7th
Just because you have cleavage does not mean everyone else should know that you have cleavage.

January 8th
All men have a one track mind and women have a one track mind…. It is very different tracks.

January 9th
Never depend on any man to make you complete as a person and do not try to complete any man who is incomplete.

January 10th
Are you stupid or do you just want people to think you are stupid?

January 11th
If you wear a skirt that short no one will have to wonder if you are a girl or a boy.

January 12th
Don't burn your bra…. Do you know how much it cost?

January 13th
Each day is a link in the chain of your life.

January 14th
Everyone will die but not everyone man really lives.

January 15th
The most important thing you can do for yourself
and your children is get an education....
Husbands die, lovers leave, but an education pays
the light bill.

January 16th
If you let the cat sleep in your room, you do not
have the right to complain about the cat poop in
the corner or the cat hair. That is what cats do.

January 17th
Compliments are said for the benefits of those
saying it not those hearing it.   Next time someone
tells you that you look just like your dad and that
mom is beautiful... say thank you... and move on.

January 18th
It is OK to have crazy relatives.... Just don't act
like them.

January 19th
Remember, no matter how good things are today, it
can always be better tomorrow or it could be
worse.... So make the most of today.

January 20th
Your dad was my best friend... your husband
should be your best friend. If you can not love and
trust the father of your children... who can you
trust?

January 21st
Life is what you make, so make it the best you can.

January 22nd
If you think that boy is great looking, look at his dad.... If his dad is a failure and ugly....chances are really good that he will be the same. Always remember apples do not fall far from the tree... neither do boys.

January 23rd
Remember, no matter how old you are or what you have accomplished there is no place like home.

January 24th
Listen to what I am saying; you do not have to do what I tell you.... Just listen to what I am telling you then you can feel guilty later that you did not follow my instructions when you see that I am right.

January 25th
When you marry, your husband is the head of the family, but you are the head of him. Give him good advice, lots of love and respect his right to be a person separate from you.... But not too far.

January 26th
It is OK to wear high heels and Channel #5 and nothing else when your husband comes home after a long job assignment....unless he brings company.

January 27th
It is a bad practice to bring wild animals into the house.

January 28th
Never do anything that you would feel uncomfortable explaining to a judge or to your children.

January 29th

Here is the test to find whether your mission on Earth is finished: if you're alive, it isn't.

January 30th

Your brother is the closest thing to honesty that you will ever have. He has no reason to tell you anything but the truth. After I am gone, listen to him. He knows what I would tell you.

January 31st

Your cousin Doris is smart, your cousin Mary Faye is athletic.... You are who you are. Don't try to be them, try to be your best you.

February 1st
It is OK to be wrong and it is OK to be right.... It is not OK not to know the difference.

February 2nd
All men want the same thing just like all women want the same thing.... The trouble is that it is not the same thing.

February 3rd
Know who you are and what you stand for and always, always listen to your mother even when she is not there.

February 4th
Never try to be rational with an irrational person.

February 5th
Sometimes less is more... with words, make-up, not with short skirts.

February 6th
If a friend tells you gossip about another friend, she will also gossip about you...and she is not a good friend.

February 7th
The formula for life is quite simple. You get up in the morning and you go to bed at night. In between, you stay busy as best you can.

February 8th

Never pick on someone who is weaker than you because that is cruel. Never pick on someone stronger that you, that is dumb. In fact, never pick on anyone because it is rude.

February 9th

You can always judge a tree by the fruit it bares... My reputation is in your hands.

February 10th

If you don't want to be eaten by an alligator, don't swim in the river.

February 11th

God put me in charge of you because he knew I would not mislead you, so listen to your mother.

February 12th

Life and Death are parts of the circle of life. It is what you do in between is the part that makes you special.

February 13th

Just because I did not tell you not to do something, does not mean you have permission to do it. THINK first, do later.

February 14th

When you are not sure what to do, plant flowers or tend a garden. It will make the world a pretty place and you will have a chance to think things through.

February 15th
Idle hands are the devil's workshop...

February 16th
Beauty does not last, ugliness does.

February 17th
You can always trust the voice in your head...It is your mother's voice.

February 18th
If you fall off a horse and break your hip, it is not the horse's fault. It is your fault for getting on the horse.

February 19th
Don't play with matches in the hay barn.

February 20th
You only have one brother left, take care of him. He will do likewise with you.

February 21st
If you wear dangling ear rings, smoke, and drink beer in public, people will think you have low morals.

February 22nd
There is no happier place to be than home with those you love.

February 23rd
Treasure those that love you and those that you love. If you are truly blessed, they will be the same people.

February 24th
If you want to eat an elephant, take one bite at a time. Eventually, you will have no elephant.

February 25th
The purpose of life is a life of purpose.

February 26th
Smile, it may not help you but it helps those who are looking at you.

February 27th
Be thoughtful of others' feelings and be forgiving of their mistakes.

February 28th
NO. It means, NO...not maybe, not perhaps, not yes... No means NO, so get over it and move on with your life.

February 29th
If you are embarrassed about being too thin, one day you will remember thinking that and will wish you still were.

March 1st

Keep a journal or write poetry.... It is fun and good exercise for an active mind.

March 2nd

Being left handed does not give you an excuse not doing things right.

March 3rd

Please don't grow-up to be the weird old lady who lives alone, crochets, and has 20 cats.

March 4th

You do not live in England; do not drive on the left side of the road....

March 5th

Do not be late for an appointment that is rude and annoying.

March 6th

Your hands are the first thing someone touches, so take care of your hands. Remember you are not a field hand even though you act like it most of the time.

March 7th

Freckles are cuter than wrinkles.

March 8th

Never be afraid to tell your mother the truth.... Be afraid if you do not.

March 9th

Chickens are not good house pets; please keep your rooster outside unlesyou want me to fry him for dinner.

March 10th

Just because you think that you know everything does not mean that you do.

March 11th

You have permission to lie to your husband about two things—your age and your weight. He knows you are lying but loves you enough to let you get by with it...even when you are not 39 and 117 pounds.

March 12th

Boyfriends are like buses.... If you miss one, you can catch the next one.

March 13th

Never go to bed angry, you may not wake up.

March 14th

Pick your husband with the same criteria that you would use to choose a best friend because he is suppose to be.

March 15th
Never be too busy to say "I love you" to someone that you love.

March 16th
There is nothing so bad or traumatic that a hug from your mom, a piece of cake and a glass of milk can't make better.

March 17th
Cats are not people. Don't ask too much from them.

March 18th
Be a good steward of your money when you are young and it will take care of you when you are old.

March 19th
Never spoil your children. They do not out grow it. Love your children. They will not out grow it

March 20th
Never flirt with a married man. He will take it the wrong way.

March 21st
That boy is too self involved. The last time I saw him he was walking down the street holding his own hand.

March 22nd
Never be loud in public, people will think you are crude.

March 23rd
Be the kind of person that you would want your own children to be.

March 24th
There should never be a day that passes without telling someone you love how much they mean to you... especially your mom.

March 25th
I am not your friend, I am your mother, but I am the best friend you will ever have.

March 26th
Never stop having quality time with your husband. Enjoy all the time that you have and help him be his best at all things.

March 27th
Multiple marriages equal multiple mistakes.

March 28th
Health should not be taken for 'granite' but sometimes a second piece of pie is mighty good.

March 29th
Why do you ask WHY when you already know the answer to the question, WHY?

March 30th
Just because the music is loud does not mean that the music is good.

March 31st
Some things are more important than others. Know the difference.

April 1st

The cats will be glad when you become a nurse so that you will stop practicing bandages on them and leave them alone.

April 2nd

One day you will thank me for what I am telling you. I hope I live long enough to hear see it.

April 3rd

When you do not know what you should do, it is OK to do nothing.

April 4th

Sometimes it is best to STOP and THINK before you do something.

April 5th

If you fall out of the tree and break both of your legs, don't come running into the house to me.

April 6th

I think people should have to apply for a license to have children. It is harder to do than driving a car.

April 7th

Can you count to three? GOOD. Give me three reasons why you would want to do what you just did.

April 8th
Mothers always love their children; they just don't always like them.

April 9th
Life is like a flower garden. Watch out for weeds and bloom wherever you are planted.

April 10th
Everyone has an opinion, I give you facts.

April 11th
The hand that rocks the cradle may rule the world, but she is sleep deprived much of the time.

April 12th
It is never too late to do your best.

April 13th
If you know that what you are doing is wrong or not good for you, don't do it.

April 14th
Giving into peer pressure is indicative of not being able to make up your own mind. You have a mind of your own, use it.

April 15th

"No matter where you wander or where you roam, be happy and healthy and glad to come home."

April 16th

God sees everything you do. I see most of everything you do. What I miss, he tells me about it.

April 17th

It does not matter if your teacher has bad breath. You are not there to smell her breath; you are there to learn from her.

April 18th

Spare the rod, spoil the Sharon.

April 19th

It is bad manners to hit your father's toe with a hammer. Life is not a cartoon.

April 20th

One day you will have children.... Time has its own revenge.

April 21st

People who use profanity are deficient in the Queen's English and have difficulty expressing what they wish to convey.

April 22nd
Just because you are loud does not mean you are right.

April 23rd
Schools have dress codes so that the teachers can teach. Boys and male teachers get distracted by short skirts and tight shirts. They know you are a girl; you do not have to prove it.

April 24th
Easy come, easy go.... Hard to get back once it is gone.

April 25th
Life and love is fragile like an egg shell. Treat both gently and with respect.

April 26th
Don't act stupid, it may become a habit.

April 27th
Yes, it is my job to make you miserable, as well as safe, happy and well adjusted.

April 28th
Bathroom scales do not lie, but mirrors do. Sometimes you see what you want to see, not what is there.

April 29th
The best advice that I can give you is to listen to your mother.

April 30th
Because I am your mother, that is why.

May 1st
Never be too proud to ask for help if you need it.

May 2nd
Life does not have to be fair, but you do.

May 3rd
Life is like a mountain road with lots of curves and hills. You may not know what is coming around the next bend so pay attention.

My 4th
Rejoice in each season of the year. Each one brings something new and exciting for your pleasure.

May 5th
Nothing makes a mother happier than to see her children happy.

May 6th
No matter where you go or what you do, your mother will always love you. That does not mean you can do something that you know is wrong.

May 7th
I love you... remember it. One day that may be the most important thing that I have ever told you.

May 8th
A dusty house is not more important than time you can spend with your family.

May 9th
Friends come and Friends go...Good friends keep coming back...

May 10th
If you put all of your eggs in one basket, keep an eye on that basket.

May 11th
You could put a Sunday dress on a pig, but it would still be a pig. The pig would not like the dress or you for putting the dress on it.

May 12th
Remember the KISS theory in life. **K**eep **I**t **S**imple **S**haron.

May 13th
There was never a good war or a bad peace.

May 14th
Work as if you had 100 years to live; pray like you will die tomorrow.

May 15th
One day with someone you LOVE is worth two tomorrows alone.

May 16th
That, which does not kill you, makes you stronger.

May 17th
There are only two things that a child shares willingly - communicable diseases and her mother's age.

May 18th
The most important thing a mother can do for her children is to love their father and the most important thing that a father can do for his children is to love the mother. It will build a strong foundation for the children to have a loving home.

May 19th
Never take parenting lightly; it is your contribution to mankind and to God.

May 20th
Don't leave your children money. Leave them happy memories that make them smile when they think of you.

May 21st
Grandchildren are OK, but if you did not do a good job with your own children why do you think they will be good parents?

24

May 22ⁿᵈ

Your cousin is a two-year-old boy. When he visits, it is kind of like having a blender on high without a top on it.

May 23ʳᵈ

A girl's best friend is her mother, but she is a mother first and friend when the daughter needs her to be.

May 24ᵗʰ

Never ask a child their opinion on any subject unless you want to hear it.

May 25ᵗʰ

No matter how old a mother becomes, she watches her children for signs of improvement.

May 26ᵗʰ

Always be slow to anger. He who angers you conquers you.

May 27ᵗʰ

Your mother is not here for you to lean on. She is here to make leaning on her unnecessary.

May 28ᵗʰ

When the child is happy, the mother is happy.
When the mother is happy, the father is happy.
When the father is happy, the child is happy... Do you see a pattern here?

25

May 29th

If boredom is the mother of invention, then you are not bored, you just need to go out and invent something.

May 30th

Sometimes I think life is just a collection of short stories pretending to be a novel.

May 31st

It you get home alive, and then it was a successful trip.

June 1st
Everyone believes in something, put God first, family second, and work third. Everything else will find its place in the scheme of things.

June 2nd
God created man and said, "This is good, but I can do better," then he made woman. He then said, "This is much better! I will put her in charge of the future." This is how mothering started.

June 3rd
You pick your friends, you pick your clothes, you pick your career, but you do not get to pick your relatives.

June 4th
Chance makes our parents; choices make our friends. Make good choices.

June 5th
Sometimes it is best to just sit down, shut up, look and listen to what is happening around you.

June 6th
Every statement does not require a response. Sometimes saying nothing will say everything.

June 7th
You do not have to like your mother, but you do have to love her. It is required.

June 8th
The only way to have a friend is to be one.

June 9th
Money can not buy happiness, but poverty does not provide happiness either.

June 10th
If you are happy and you have money, enjoy it, share it, and be a good steward of it.

June 11th
Honor your father and mother so that your days will be long on this earth (Bible) and if you keep it up, I will personally shorten your days.

June 12th
A mother is someone who knows you well, but loves you just the same.

June 13th
Families not only live in harmony, but also in melody.

June 14th
Any one can sing, you just make a joyful noise. Remember, you are good at math so you do not have to depend on singing to make a living.

June 15th
Insanity does not run in that boy's family. It gallops like a herd of wild horses.

June 16th
Never be ashamed of your family or embarrassed. They are what make you who you are, be grateful that they are part of you.

June 17th
The reason that grandchildren and grandparents get along so well is that they have a common enemy. I can not wait until you have children.

June 18th
Don't take life too seriously; you will never get out of it alive.

June 19th
If that was my child, I would go to church under an assumed name.

June 20th
Don't act like a fool because people will think that you are one.

June 21st
Your behavior is so loud that I can hear what you are saying.

June 22nd
Keep your work ethic, it will provide an example for others and a role model for your children.

June 23rd
Respect ... give it to those that deserve it, have earned it, and those who need it.

June 24th
One day when you look into the mirror, you will know that the most important gift I have given you is your eyes and how you see the world through them.

June 25th
Pray for those that you love and those that you don't.

June 26th
It is OK to not have all of the answers to all of the questions that you are asked.

June 27th
Never be too busy to live your life and enjoy it.

June 28th
Remember no matter where you go, there you are.

June 29th
There is a little bad in the best of us and a little good in the worst of us.

June 30th
Don't ask a question if you do not want to know the answer.

July 1st

Intelligence is hard to measure – stupid isn't.

July 2nd

If you are doing is not working; stop doing it. Study the situation and change what you are doing.

July 3rd

Know who you are.

July 4th

Don't just know your strengths and weaknesses, understand them.

July 5th

Never hide your candle under a bush. You'll catch the bush on fire and loose your candle.

July 6th

Just because you avoid confrontation does not mean it will avoid you.

July 7th

Don't trouble trouble until trouble troubles you.

July 8th
Have an attitude of gratitude.

July 9th
It doesn't really matter what you think if you do not do anything with the thoughts.

July 10th
You can not inspire others if you are not inspired.

July 11th
If you want to know more, you can. If you want to know less, you can't because you already know it.

July 12th
It is a big world out there even if you never leave your hometown.

July 13th
Just because you take your bat and ball and come home does not mean that the game is over. You are just not in it anymore.

July 14th
If you do not know where you are you can't go where you want to be.

July 15th
Just because it is not your fault does not mean that you do not have to do something about it.

July 16th
No one lives forever, so use the time that you have. You are not going to get anymore.

July 17th
When the chips are down and times are tough, who you are will be obvious to those around you.

July 18th
Changing your clothes does not change who you are but it does make you easier to look at.

July 19th
I was 41 when you were born. No one else needs to know that even if they ask.

July 20th
Just because there is a hurricane happening does not mean that the cows do not have to be milked and feed.

July 21st
Think of your mind like an umbrella. It can not protect you from the elements unless it is opened.

July 22nd
How often should you tell someone that you love them? You tell them every second of every day by the things you do not just the words that you say.

July 23rd
Life is like a ladder. You have to climb it one rung (step) at a time if you want to get to the top of it.

July 24th
Everyone needs to feel accepted and acceptable. Treat them that way and they will respond in like kind.

July 25th
Doing nothing is not doing nothing. It is deciding not to do what you know you should be doing.

July 26th
Never forget to plan ahead. The journey of Life needs a roadmap.

July 27th
Take comfort from being with those that you love.

July 28th
Everyone gets tired, so that is not an excuse for not finishing what you start.

July 29th
If you play on the road, don't be surprised if you get run over by a car.

July 30th
I heard you and I am choosing not to answer a question when I know that you know the answer.

July 31st
Never ask your brother if you look good in a dress unless you want to hear the truth.

August 1st
You may not be your brother's keeper but he is yours.

August 2nd
Team work begins at home.

August 3rd
If you do not take care of your husband, someone else will.

August 4th
Prepare for the future but don't forget to take care of now.

August 5th
Be grateful for your health, wealth, and your happiness. Take care of all three.
(My Mother's Birthday!)

August 6th
Birds and Bees? "Birds want to lay eggs and bees want make honey. Girls wear short skirts to attract men with money. Eggs become birds and bees will sting. Men will take what they want and not leave a thing."

August 7th
It is better to make a good life than a good living, but it is best to do both.

August 8th
Just because you are tired of listening does not mean that I am tired of talking.

August 9th
Freedom is not being free it is being able to think and act accordingly.

August 10th
You can control yourself, not others.

August 11th
When you are not sure what to do, don't do anything.

August 12th
Never yell at children or animals. It will make them nervous and they will not trust you and you will end up getting hurt.

August 13th
If you want someone to do something ask them. If you want them to know how to do something, show them. If you want them to screw it up, make them do something.

August 14th
It is not a new world, it is the same world it has always been and the rules have not changed.

August 15th
It is good to have friends but you do not have to talk to them on the phone every minute of the day.

August 16th
Men are similar to cars. Some have 8 cylinders, some may have 4, some are made for families, some aren't. Pick your husband with the more care you would use to choose a new car. Know what you want and you need and remember; it is easier to trade a car than a husband.

August 17th
Cats are not people, too. They are cats and that is obvious if you observe their behavior.

August 18th
If you teach a man to fish, he will go fishing. Teach him to cook a fish and he will make a mess in the kitchen.

August 19th
Never sell yourself short, in fact, never sell yourself period.

August 20th
Love is not love until you give it away.

August 21st
It is OK to love someone from a distance, just don't follow them around. It will make them think you are weird.

August 22nd

If you want a boy to talk to you, you talk to him. If he does not want to talk, he will let you know.

August 23rd

Your cousin is young but he has the character of man who will do his best at everything. Wait and see him in 20 years, you will be impressed.

August 24th

There is nothing more important than your family and remember, I am your family, too.

August 25th

One day you will have a daughter and I am going to laugh out loud at you.

August 26th

Grandparents and grandchildren have a common enemy.

August 27th

You are too young to think about getting married, you do not remember to feed the cat. How are you going to cook dinner for a husband who has been at work all day?

August 28th

Just because you are old enough to drive a car does not mean that you should be driving a car.

August 29th

Do you ever get tired of doing what everyone else is doing? It is OK to be yourself and not follow the pack.

August 30th

There is nothing better than ice cream on the porch on a hot Saturday night with someone that you love.

August 31st

Keep your children close to your heart but keep your husband closer.

September 1st
Give him a kidney? I would not give him the time of day.

September 2nd
There is a reason why crazy people act crazy. It is because they are crazy. Stay away from crazy people.

September 3rd
If a boy asks you to do something because he loves you and you love him, tell him you are doing something for him...you are going home.

September 4th
It is OK to laugh at your self just not in public and not too often.

September 5th
It is true that fish live in schools but did you ever see one graduate?

September 6th
If you want to have sex with a boy, don't talk to him for 30 days and observe his behavior. If he replaces you with another girl, you will know that he did not love you just the want to get laid. You will be glad that you did not sleep with him.

September 7th
There is nothing more urgent than being a teenage girl.

September 8th
Being a teenager is a temporary inconvenience on the journey of a lifetime.

September 9th
Being a teenager with a problem is like a car with a flat tire. Just fix the damn thing and keep going.

September 10th
I understand why some cats eat their kittens when they are born.

September 11th
Horses are wonderful when they are well trained. Come to think of it, so are children.

September 12th
Take care of your saddle and your equipment. It will keep you safe.

September 13th
Don't expect the horse to think for you, it is your job to think for him.

September 14th
Just because something costs more does not mean it is better.

September 15th
Look before you leap. In fact, you do not always have to leap.

September 16th
Just because you can....does not mean you should.

September 17th
Just because you do not know something does not mean that someone else does not know it.

September 18th
Pick your battles and pick your wars. More important, pick your strategy and your weapons carefully.

September 19th
Turkeys are for thanksgiving dinner not for dating.

September 20th
If a boy does not have manners at the dinner table, there are probably other things missing as well.

September 21st
Never be jealous of others. If you think that they are better than you, then you should be trying to make yourself better, not wasting time on jealousy.

September 22nd
If I can see your underwear when you sit down, then it is obvious to me that the skirt is too short.

September 23rd
Never forget to say THANK YOU when someone does something nice for you and to say YOU ARE WELCOME when you are told thank you, too.

September 24th
Good behavior usually gets good behavior. The same is true for bad behavior.

September 25th
Lazy people do not become president of the United States.

September 26th
Lazy people are the results of bad parenting.

September 27th
Lazy people have lazy children. Guess it is genetic because the same is true for hard working people.

September 28th
Never judge someone by their religious convictions and beliefs, if you must judge them, judge them for not having them.

September 29th
If you don't plant the seeds, don't expect them to grow.

September 30th
Flower gardens are like children, they need a lot of tending.

October 1ˢᵗ
His grandmother and grandfather had to get married. His mom and dad had to get married. You are surprised that he had to get married?

October 2ⁿᵈ
Apples never fall far from the tree.

October 3ʳᵈ
Cats and dogs do not like playing school and are not going to sit still no matter what you tell them.

October 4ᵗʰ
Spring smells like a new beginning.

October 5ᵗʰ
If you have rat snakes in the barn, then you have rats.

October 6ᵗʰ
Even if you complain, you still have to do your chores, so save energy and be quiet.

October 7ᵗʰ
Boys and girls are not the same and they are not equal. In the legal system, they have the same rights, but they are not treated equally there either.

October 8th

Pretty people are better than ugly people. Thinner people are better than fat people. White people are treated better than black people. Men are treated better than women. If you believe any of that, then you have not been listening to me the last two decades. You get what you give.

October 9th

Make love not war... How about make your bed and not play your music so loud?

October 10th

Slow and steady leads the way.... Just don't quit before you get to the end of the job.

October 11th

You can change who you are but you can change what you do.

October 12th

There is no such think as luck. It is opportunities taken.

October 13th

Believe in something. Have a code for your life.

October 14th

How does a bird build a nest? It takes one straw at a time and weaves it into her home. Memories are woven into your memory to help you know how to build your home.

October 15th
Right and wrong are not points of view. One is right and one is wrong. Do you get my point?

October 16th
I love a clean house especially when I come home and find one.

October 17th
If you make a mess, clean it up. Just because I gave birth to you does not mean that the labor continues throughout your life.

October 18th
If it is broken, fix it. If it is not broken, please don't fix it.

October 19th
Basketballs and lamps do not belong in the same room.... Unless you want to buy me a new lamp.

October 20th
Credit cards will kill a budget faster than a bullet in the head.

October 21st
You want a car. Start a savings account and one day you can buy one.

October 22nd

Be careful little feet where you go. Be careful little hands what you do. Be careful little ears what you hear. Be careful little eyes what you see and be careful little mouth what you say. Be careful in all that you do.

October 23rd

If you do not want to step in the manure, stay out of the field.

October 24th

Respect yourself. You only get one you.

October 25th

Life is not like the piano. You do not get to practice lots of times before you get it right.

October 26th

Classical music is like expensive wine. Some are good and some are crap.

October 27th

I don't have many days left, so I am going to make them count. You should live every day of your life that way.

October 28th

There is nothing on earth stronger than the bond between a mother and her children.

October 29th
Even though the umbilical cord has been cut, you are still part of me and I am part of you.

October 30th
I will always be there for you even when I am not.

October 31st
I regret not having more children so that I could have had more grandchildren.

November 1st
You taught your nephew to love music. His parents reinforced it. He will always have a song in his heart and you helped put it there.

November 2nd
Your sister in law is not just your sister in law, she is your friend and your sister.

November 3rd
Life is not a bowl of cherries, Life is what you do everyday and how you do it.

November 4th
Don't just keep the Bible on your desk, read it from time to time. You might just learn something.

November 5th
Hug your friends and treasure your time with them.

November 6th
If cleanliness is next to godliness, I know a lot of people who are going straight to hell.

November 7th
You could have made another cat from all of the cat hair on her sofa.

November 8th
Your Aunt Sally is the nicest person in the entire family. Her home is clean, her mind is clear, her children are polite. She is even nice to stray dogs and cats. If you want to be like someone, be like her not Janis Joplin.

November 9th
It is OK to be OK. Relax and enjoy it.

November 10th
If you are allergic to something, leave it alone.

November 11th
Just because your appendix ruptured does not mean you do not have to go to class.

November 12th
OK, you graduated from high school. Now you will graduate from nursing school, then you go to graduate school... are you seeing a pattern? You are never finished learning. Graduating from high school is the baby step into your educational processes.

November 13th
If that bikini was any smaller, you would be arrested for public nudity.

November 14th
Yoga has made me more physically flexible and having a child at 41 made me mentally flexible.

November 15th
Be like a rubber ball... You can bounce back and the harder you hit the ground the higher you can bounce back.

November 16th
Wash your hair, put on your make-up, and wear a pretty dress. Even if you do not leave the house, you will feel special.

November 17th
Don't ever do anything in excess except love.

November 18th
Dance with your children. After your children are in bed, dance with your husband.

November 19th
Don't ever let your husband or children come home to an unhappy home.

November 20th
If you do not have a husband or children when you grow up, you can still have a happy home.

November 21st
You can not control other people's thoughts or behavior but you can influence them.

November 22nd
Lead by example.

November 23ʳᵈ
Be your best in all that you do.

November 24ᵗʰ
Never be too busy to walk barefoot in the grass but watch out for fire ant beds.

November 25ᵗʰ
When you go to college, I will not miss you. Your time with me has ended. It makes me happy to know that you are following a dream and have a path for your life.

November 26ᵗʰ
You have grown from just being my daughter to being my friend.

November 27ᵗʰ
Never believe anyone who blames other people for their own bad behavior.

November 28ᵗʰ
Everyone has their own path to follow.

November 29ᵗʰ
Dream and work to make your dreams reality.

November 30ᵗʰ
Remember three things: where you came from and
where you are going, and where you are.

December 1st
Go to church to find your place in the universe.
Pray to find your place on earth.

December 2nd
I do not believe in atheists. All dying people believe
in GOD and want his help. Don't wait to the last
minute to contact him.

December 3rd
Even if you do not believe in GOD, he believes in
you.

December 4th
There is nothing more beautiful than a dad, mom,
and new baby together in their own home.

December 5th
Raise your children the way you want them to be
and they will not stray from it especially if you live
the example.

December 6th
Old people have special needs, mostly to be loved
and appreciated.

December 7th
Be the person that you want your husband to be.

December 8th
Keep a journal of the happy times in your life.

December 9th
My parents understood me and I understand you.... You will understand your kids. It will freak them out.

December 10th
Flower Power means having a nice garden that grows back each year. Plant lots of Lantana.

December 11th
Do you believe in magic? Make those green beans disappear.

December 12th
If you make your cousins eat your food so that you can go outside, the only thing you are getting out of this is fat cousins.

December 13th
It is easier to do it right the first time.

December 14th
Listen to your mother and follow her lead.

December 15th
If I tell you something is really, really dumb, it probably is.

December 16th
I think that you are wonderful. I hope one day you will think the same of me.

December 17th
Tell your children about their grandmother and make sure that they know how to cook, clean, and love....not necessarily in that order.

December 18th
Kiss your children goodnight for me and tell your husband that if you are a good wife, it is because you had a good mother.

December 19th
Please do not spend your whole life with only horses and cats.

December 20th
It is better to watch the news than to be on it.

December 21st
If you eat only carrots, you will turn orange.

December 22nd

Your father can not be with you, so he left you two uncles. It takes two uncles to equal one daddy.

December 23rd

Uncles are people, too. So are aunts.

December 24th

I know lots of things, so you should listen to me. Some of those things might be the bit of information that you have been seeking.

December 25th

When I say grow up, I do not want you to do it too fast.

December 26th

I hope your children get along as well as you and your brother.... Yes, I know what that means..... ha, ha, ha....

December 27th

Your father was the perfect man for me. I hope you blessed the same way.

December 28th

Never say something mean just because you can. It will come back on you every time.

December 29th
Understand where others are starting and you can help them get to where they need to be.

December 30th
There can not be a future without a present and a past.

December 31st
Each day is not a new beginning, it is a continuation of your life.

H A P P Y   N E W   Y E A R !

www.ingramcontent.com/pod-product-compliance
Lightning Source LLC
Chambersburg PA
CBHW050821290526
45792CB00001B/205